The Collection 2011

The Collection 2011

EXPRESS NEWSPAPERS

hamlyn

An Hachette UK Company
www.hachette.co.uk

First published in Great Britain in 2010 by
Hamlyn, a division of Octopus Publishing Group Ltd
Endeavour House
189 Shaftesbury Avenue
London
WC2H 8JY
www.octopusbooks.co.uk

Cartoon selection by John Field

ISBN 978-0-600-62119-5

A CIP catalogue record for this book is available from the British Library

Printed and bound in India by Gopsons Papers Ltd.

1 3 5 7 9 10 8 6 4 2

Contents

An Introduction by
Lee Latchford Evans

My childhood memories will never fade as long as my collection of Giles annuals sits on my study shelves. I remember always getting the newest edition for Christmas. It became a tradition, it was expected, each book full of a year's worth of funny scenes and endearing characters. It was a treasure trove of exciting clips that I could lose myself in and imagine I were there in the frames.

The most famous of all Giles's characters was Grandma, a grumpy difficult old lady with a distinctive hat and umbrella (my manager sometimes reminds me of Grandma!).

I've read that Giles was a perfectionist and liked to spend up to six hours on a single drawing so the detail became a huge part of the entertainment value. I recall scenes with animals and all of them had their own characters; each individual animal was just as important to Giles as the other. I liked to look out for the little extra characters almost hidden in the background of his cartoons – they might be small but were full of life and are so important to the overall story being told by the picture.

Giles drew thousands of cartoons spanning generations – he drew history. He was a true inspiration to the creative mind and a real genius, appreciated by people wanting to learn about the world around them. He has left us a wonderful legacy, a colourful portrait of history, which we can continue to enjoy for years to come. I am one of his greatest fans. Thank you Giles!

Lee Latchford Evans
Formerly of Steps

Politics

And here we have Ernie doing a spot of bookmaker's running for Clem...

Daily Express, October 13, 1949

"Ernie reckons we ought to see if this Brumas can draw a full attendance in the House."

Daily Express, April 11, 1950

"Sending Webb Valentines won't get you more meat than anyone else."

Daily Express, February 13, 1951

"Don't be silly, Ernie – nobody's been arranging peace conferences behind your back."

Sunday Express, March 4, 1951

"Et tu, Harold?"

Daily Express, April 24, 1951

"Here is a police message – Shortly after the opening of the Festival the Skylon on the South Bank was reported missing. Anyone who can give information..."

Sunday Express, May 6, 1951

"Don't look now Tito, I think we're being followed."

Sunday Express, July 29, 1951

"How d'you like that – Joe and Vishinsky called at No.10 for a peace conference – didn't know I was out."

Daily Express, January 6, 1952

"When you say 'Well DONE,' do you refer to Mr. Butler or us?"

Daily Express, January 30, 1952

"Of course I'm confident of victory – it's the inclusion of the unfortunate terms 'had it' that gives me the occasional twinge."

Daily Express, October 6, 1959

"I'm afraid we must face it, m'lady – having asked him to open our Fete as a Cabinet Minster,
we're stuck with him as a back-bencher."

Daily Express, July 17, 1962

"No, it isn't true we've come to Moscow because, if we mention
Ban the Bomb in London, they put us in vans and whoosh – away we go."

Daily Express, July 16, 1963

"On the other hand, if you *don't* all get out and let him count you yon Polls will be closed."

Daily Express, November 7, 1963

"I think it was a mistake to thump him because he bit you when you kissed him."

Sunday Express, September 27, 1964

"*I* didn't say you had a pretty poor mentality you thickheaded bunch of numbskulls."

Sunday Express, October 4, 1964

"I wouldn't be surprised if our impartial commentary on Rhodesia is going to be just a little teeny weeny bit biased in favour of Mr. Smith."

Daily Express, October 5, 1965

"And I move, Mr. President, that it would be kinda cute to erect a statue of our brave veteran hero – hijacker Raffaele Minichiello."

Daily Express, November 4, 1969

"That's for twisting my wrist when you presented me with that honorary degree last Saturday."

Daily Express, November 2, 1971

"Never mind Mancroft, it'll be all right on the day."

Daily Express, October 26, 1972

"Nab, before you let off any more hot air about Opposition Leader's obnoxious habit of smoking..."

Daily Express, 13 February, 1973

"That's a nice turn up for the book, Pop, 'Future Labour M.P. opens Conservative Fete'."

Sunday Express, June 10, 1973

"Careful with this one – he had Jeremy Thorpe yesterday."

Daily Express, 12 February, 1974

"Buying my secretary chocolates every day may well be considered
as a bribe in high places."

Daily Express, May 2, 1974

"She's just had a tenner on the old 7 to 4 on, Ted."

Daily Express, February 4, 1975

"What he's really saying is 'Maggie, I know a little shop that will let you have as many crates of tinned food as you can store at 10 per cent off'."

Daily Express, February 11, 1975

"He's never bitten anybody before – it's just that he don't like jubilant Tories."

Sunday Express, November 7, 1976

"Just what the doctor ordered – Moscow wants to
enter a yacht in the America's Cup race!"

Daily Express, April 15, 1980

"Only a fool like you would ask his father why so many people want to be President of the United States."

Daily Express, April 29, 1980

Daily Express, November 4, 1980

"Brighton air does something for them – not one Mr. Smith among 'em so far."

Daily Express, October 5, 1982

"Now don't do anything Mr. Pym tells you to unless Mrs. Thatcher says you can."

Daily Express, May 14, 1985

"First I saw Clark Gable as Mr. Christian, then Ted Heath as Mr. Christian."

Daily Express, 16 May 1985

"Very unfortunate, Boris – you just stuck your testing-pin in Mr. Gorbachev."

Sunday Express, August 3, 1986

" 'Wouldn't vote for a MP with a dial like that!' Some of the electorate haven't peeped in the old magic mirror on the wall, lately."

Daily Express, February 26, 1987

"Sorry, Mr. Homes, Dr. Watson – I didn't realise you were working for the Inland Revenue."

Sunday Express, October 25, 1987

Sporting moments

"Any truth in the rumour that you boys are organising a relief fund for distressed dog track owners?"

Daily Express, November 14, 1947

"I ain't loitering – I've fallen head over tip."

Daily Express, April 18, 1951

"Dad won't find much to bet with in *my* money-box – I've put it on Gordon Richards already."

Sunday Express, May 27, 1951

Late arrival at Epsom on the grounds that if the French can run horses in the Derby, so can any member of the Western bloc.

Daily Express, May 28, 1952

"The sooner you get to Helsinki out of here the better."

Daily Express, July 18, 1952

"As yours seems to be the only halfpenny-nap team entered I would say you stand a very good chance of winning."

Daily Express, July 27, 1952

"Not just now, men – I'm expecting a call from the Express."

Daily Express, May 10, 1955

THE GILES FAMILY arrived at Silverstone yesterday in their caravan-studio for what Grandma calls "a few days' peace and quiet in the pits." To those who know the deafening row that goes with motor-racing, "peace and quiet" will seem strange words to describe the non-stop roaring, revving, backfiring, and hollering of the pits. But Grandma says she prefers the deafening din of the pits at meal times which drowns the deafening din of the twins, etc., sorting out their dozens of different cereals and pots of jam and this and that.

A further report of the family at Silverstone is due this page tomorrow.

Prelude to Silverstone...

Daily Express, September 12, 1957

"The MCC sacking Wardle for saying rude things is one thing – sacking the Vicar for calling us a bunch of incompetent silly mid-ons in his Parish Magazine is another."

Daily Express, August 21, 1958

"Follow main route through town, bear left and over unguarded crossing – that was a near one – proceed uphill to next major road junction..."

Daily Express, January 20, 1959

"Pater – what price Mamma's Anglo-Soviet relationship if the Russians walk away with it?"

Daily Express, July 21, 1959

"At least it's put some life in the blessed game."

Sunday Express, April 10, 1960

"Double Sir Winston's reward for its recapture and bring me a brush."

Daily Express, February 16, 1961

"I don't know why the Russians are making a fuss about a little extra weight – I always get rid of all mine at the first fence."

Daily Express, March 3, 1961

"It took just one day's racing at Ayr to blue my First World War gratuity of £97.
What had taken three and a half years to earn as a soldier, four races at Ayr wiped out."

Daily Express, March 25, 1963

"Please can we have our ball?"

Daily Express, May 11, 1963

"Overtaking at 185 miles an hour, cornering at 93 miles an hour, no silencer – oh dear, Mr. Marples isn't going to like this."

Daily Express, May 11, 1963

"Hullo, Murgatroyd – what's your sick aunt you had the day off to visit backing in the next race?"

Daily Express, March 17, 1964

"Relax, sonny – we're not going to fix your Tote – we're just looking the joint over with a view to purchase."

Daily Express, July 3, 1964

"Funny to think he's the chairman of Save the World's Wildlife."

Daily Express, September 22, 1964

"Let anyone ask *me* to skip the beauty of breeze and sail to open the Commonwealth Games in Jamaica..."

Daily Express, August 4, 1966

"All we want now is for him to take up grouse shooting."

Daily Express, August 12, 1971

"Completing your first successful jump does not entitle you to give Miss. Ringboane a Harvey Smith salute, Angela."

Daily Express, August 19, 1971

"Oh! Er – hullo there – Harvey."

Daily Express, July 18, 1972

"Mr. Oxley, if you think the 'Queen's little boy' got tough with you, stay under cover – here comes his Dad."

"O.K. Lou – if you don't want a repeat of this get in here, mingle unobtrusively and pick up the players' form."

Daily Express, June 20, 1975

"If we had a skipper who wasn't so preoccupied with the annihilation of Kerry Packer, we might have been higher in the charts for the Admiral's Cup."

Daily Express, August 3, 1977

"The cricket-mad British have not quite got your awareness of impending doom, my Lord."

Daily Express, January 18, 1978

"Archibald reckons that as he's the only non-ASH man here he's entitled to 90 per cent of anything that's coming."

Daily Express, May 24, 1978

"One all mod-con coming up."

Daily Express, July 14, 1978

"Did I detect a flicker of a smile when Brother Huff slipped over and bumped his head?"

Daily Express, January 25, 1979

" 'Ello, ello, ello, – we can't have that sort of language 'ere, Ma'am!"

Daily Express, September 16, 1980

"Remember men – any bad language from any of them, no charging on to the green."

Daily Express, September 25, 1980

"Would it be all right if I just give him one with my fist?"

Sunday Express, August 2, 1981

"Don't start writing stories about extravagance, if Diana can afford all these new clothes,
surely Anne can have a second-hand red carpet."

Daily Express, April 23, 1985

Transport

"Never mind where I got it from – they're not getting any increased fares out of me."

Sunday Express, June 2, 1946

"I've solved your car problem – won this lot in a radio quiz."

Daily Express, June 24, 1948

"It's when they get the Queen Mary AND the Queen Elizabeth in Fleet-street the real fun will start."

Daily Express, August 25, 1949

"If Cripps don't put the bite on Wall-street for dollars, he'll put the British on vegetables to show this Peron where he gets off."

Daily Express, September 6, 1949

"Decent of Ramsbotham to accept our suggestion that in an emergency he'd be the engine."

Daily Express, February 20, 1951

"Lot of wasted talent here that could be doing us a bit of good in Cortina."

Daily Express, February 2, 1956

"He may be right, he may be wrong, but I think I preferred him when all we knew about him was his hat."

Daily Express, November 10, 1956

"My husband was saying – by the number of times you go down to the sea on basic he reckons you get 320 miles to the gallon."

Daily Express, March 5, 1957

"I think I've got it all, dear – don't lose my ticket, don't lean out of the window, don't forget to give Mr. Cousins a piece of your mind, steer clear of Trevor Evans, abolish the cost of living, don't get drunk, demand the repeal of the Rent Act..."

Daily Express, September 3, 1957

"To quote Burns: 'I wasna fou, but just had plenty'."

Daily Express, March 1, 1960

"Shall I tell Laura you piled up after a cowboy gave you a thick ear for backfiring in front of his horse?"

Daily Express, October 4, 1960

"Well I DON'T think our faithful servant is good for another year and I DO see the sense in harnessing ourselves with a new one which would only eat up petrol."

Daily Express, October 16, 1962

The taxi drivers who ordered President Kennedy's brother to the end of the rank should watch it if they try the same thing with Sir Roy Welensky.

Daily Express, February 27, 1962

"Pardon my smile, chum."

Sunday Express, May 10, 1964

"Herbert! Come in and take that thing down, at once."

Daily Express, January 18, 1966

"A right Charlie I'm going to look tomorrow: 'Sorry,
Your Majesty, but someone's sold it to a rich American'."

Daily Express, September 19, 1967

"Getting Mrs. Castle honked and selling her one of our Super Z Type Sports may not be funny or clever, but it's damn good salesmanship."

Daily Express, October 17, 1967

"This lady claims you clipped her across the ear for getting on your bus after closing time!"

Daily Express, December 12, 1968

"Ministry of Technology? So far the Concorde sonic boom has been hardly audible..."

Daily Express, September 3, 1970

"Forget the stewardess who said she'd like to drop you off at 30,000ft., Mick – Dad here says he'd make it 60,000."

Daily Express, December 2, 1971

"What, and risk being done for trespassing?"

Daily Express, March 9, 1976

"Don't ask Goldilocks in the corner what he thought of the Vote of Confidence results – I got a Harvey Smith."

Daily Express, March 29, 1979

"Harry's not soaking them with thoughts of love – he's soaking them because he can't stand their blaring radios."

Daily Express, July 30, 1987

In uniform

"Mark my words, chum, if things in England get much worse half the population will be having a go at this Overlander business."

Daily Express, August 26, 1947

"Well – this is Leap Year, my name's Gracie and he's a radio engineer..."

Daily Express, January 1, 1952

"Your innings, Mr. Hutton."

Daily Express, March 2, 1954

"Don't drop it, chum. This wonderful Russian Navy news is playing Old Harry with his gout this morning."

Daily Express, August 27, 1954

"End window, top floor – in ten minutes she'll be fifteen."

Daily Express, September 22, 1955

"Brother, when I tip-toe out of Europe you won't see my feet for dust."

Daily Express, March 12, 1957

"Trapped! Pincered by superior forces armed with countless stories of what happened in 1939. We buy the beer."

Daily Express, September 2, 1958

"Yes, gentlemen, 1940 was a very hectic time. So hectic that some of us were so anxious to do battle with the Luftwaffe we rushed off without settling for one or two outstanding drinks."

Daily Express, September 13, 1960

"Our captain says go tell your skipper that those damn tickets for the Scottish Boat Show in Glasgow don't entitle you to a free inspection of our ships."

Daily Express, March 8, 1961

My spies from the East and my special agents from the West report there is no truth in the rumour that the hordes of "refugees," having collected their ballpoint pens signed by the Vice-President of the United States, are now nipping home via the barricades enriched by this fascinating glimpse of the American way of life.

Daily Express, August 22, 1961

"Bud, I'm going to have to ask you to knock off referring to our wives as the export chicks."

Daily Express, August 13, 1963

"On guard, Romford Rockers! Retaliation raid from Clacton Trads."

Daily Express, April 2, 1964

"Inspector Barlow? Nothing to report, Sir."
(A new force of "Z Boats" may be formed to stop teenage nudists holding parties on the Thames.)

Sunday Express, July 12, 1964

"It appears that one of us has been writing to Mr. Wilson advising him to accept the £95 million then apply for compassionate leave for the whole damn B.A.O.R."

Daily Express, March 9, 1965

"Right! At parade when the C.O. warned that Mr. Wilson will almost certainly thin out the Armed Forces with the R.A.F. taking the biggest knock which one of you said 'Ooray'?"

Daily Express, July 19, 1966

"The damn dogs didn't mind it but the sentries said 'Phew'."

Daily Express, October 24, 1968

"And now, if the man who sewed St. Michael labels in Sergeant's uniform and underwear will kindly..."

Daily Express, February 18, 1969

Six civil servants from Whitehall – sign here in triplicate.

Scottish Daily Express, December 29, 1972

"Only the Press, Comrade, they heard you have a reputation for being a bit of a boy when reporters are around."

Sunday Express, September 2, 1973

"Right ho, chaps – the Royal Romance is officially denied. You will now cut cards for the privilege of ordering a whip-round for the wedding present."

Daily Express, September 25, 1973

"Music hath charms, Charlie boy."

Daily Express, October 23, 1973

"I trust the ingredients of our bangers and beans have been mixed with the same loving care as HRH's cake."

Sunday Express, November 11, 1973

"They're selling them off at the Playboy Club."

Sunday Express, November 18, 1973

"Well that's all right lads. 11.0 Matins; early lunch; kick-off 3.0; back here by 5.30; wash and brush up and a cup of tea; Evensong 6.30."

Daily Express, January 8, 1974

"For using your helmet at Twickenham for services beyond the call of duty, Her Royal Highness has commanded me to present you with a new hat."

Daily Express, April 23, 1974

"Like I said, if they ban private wards you'll have the general wards
bung full of Kings, Queens and Dooks, and all and sundry 'OUTSIDE'!"

Daily Express, November 5, 1974

"A very remarkable impersonation of Sir Charles Chaplin at the Palace, Guardsman Davies.
After his dubbing you will receive my standing ovation in the Guardhouse."

Daily Express, March 4, 1975

"These should get you at least two years, Caponi. Bert, run them round to the hospital for general release on the N.H.S."

Daily Express, February 10, 1976

"Permission to strike, Sir?"

Sunday Express, October 3, 1976

"You the one that ordered the emergency rations?"

Daily Express, January 31, 1977

"I fear yours is a case of hard luck, matey – yours being the first case of the day and your name being M. Foot."

Daily Express, May 18, 1977

"You think he's lovely is no excuse to call Prince Charles to cool our canteen dispute."

Daily Express, June 17, 1977

"The thoughts of Sir Neil Cameron get on your what, Corporal?"

Daily Express, May 3, 1978

"Scotland Yard? We got your wire to return Joyce McKinney. Guess we'll send you a batch and you can sort one out your end."

Daily Express, May 19, 1978

"One minor security risk, Sir – there could be a terrorist inside any one of 'em!"

Daily Express, July 18, 1978

"Jim doesn't think you were doing much for the 'All-pals-together.' That's his missus you're dancing with."

Daily Express, August 29, 1978

"Personally speaking, I have no objection whatsoever to the New York Irish G.I.s taking over my job."

Sunday Express, April 22, 1979

"In the next scene we cut to the U.S. Cavalry coming to the rescue down the Falls Road."

Daily Express, September 6, 1979

"Can he have a couple of dozen as souvenirs for a few of his friends back home?"

Daily Express, September 11, 1979

"Touchy aren't we – I was only joking when I said I trust you've got your warrants in order."

Daily Express, 25 March, 1986

"Some pips'll squeak if we don't get some of Nigel Lawson's surplus £6 billion."

Daily Express, January 19, 1988

Family affairs

"Fancy not finding out where the fight was before letting that gentleman sell you three ringside seats."

Daily Express, September 13, 1951

"Watch his T-square – I just suggested he did a cartoon on Maclean and Burgess marrying Princess Tiger Eyes."

Daily Express, September 20, 1955

"Lend us a couple of those Balaclavas you're knitting for the troops, Vera."

Daily Express, August 8 1956

Grandma arriving in Blackpool.

Daily Express, August 20, 1957

Grandma and Sister Lily enjoying the beach.

Daily Express, August 22, 1957

"I know one party who's not as enthusiastic as the Daily Express about little boys who build rockets in their gardens."

Daily Express, June 30, 1959

"It's one thing for Mr. Krushchev to call people 'ublyudki' but quite another for little boys to call their Grandmas 'ublyudki'."

Sunday Express, May 22, 1960

"I love it! Every time a Princess or a Prime Minister comes past –
'You can't sit there like that put a collar and tie on at once!'"

Daily Express, August 6, 1970

"That's Grandma's SOS for the day – good night party political broadcast."

Daily Express, January 24, 1974

"You are entitled to your own political beliefs regardless of race, religion or colour,
but you will kindly refrain from calling the rest of us 'Brothers'."

Sunday Express, February 10, 1974

"Dad, why do we have to have 'Scotland the Brave' all through breakfast just because Grandma's got a wee sister in Aberdeen?"

Daily Express, June 25, 1974

"Our delegation points out that they see no clause in Mr. Wilson's White Paper referring to a £6 maximum pocket money."

Sunday Express, July 13, 1975

"They're going to be one short. Vera's just voted for Jerry Ford because she felt sorry for him."

Daily Express, November 4, 1976

"Asking your MP to burn Jean Rook at the stake for not being nice about your girl friend Angela Rippon is not very democratic."

Daily Express, December 9, 1976

"We love ya, baby, you've just saved racing and the Jockey Club – your 'orse lost."

Daily Express, June 1, 1977

England expects!

Daily Express, July 4 1977

"He's got a letter from Mrs. Cholmondleigh's poodle's solicitors charging you with rape."

Daily Express, January 26, 1982

"You've won two Daily Express prizes, Grandma –
a ticket to play Steve Davis in a frame of snooker and a Princess Diana dress to go in."

Daily Express, April 30, 1985

Another great title from Hamlyn

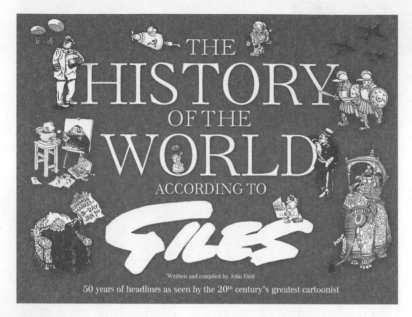
Victory celebrations 1945

On August 15, 1945, after almost six years of military conflict, which covered a large part of the globe and resulted in the deaths of many millions of people, the final step with victory over Japan brought about mass celebrations throughout the country. In this cartoon, Giles captured the widespread and spontaneous outpouring of joy in the nation's capital, where tightly packed crowds milled and danced between Buckingham Palace, Whitehall, Trafalgar Square and Piccadilly Circus.

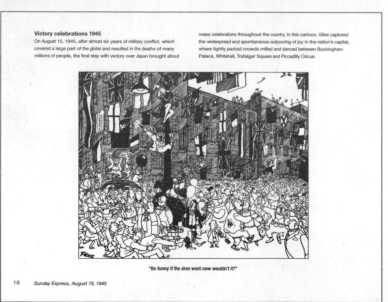

"Be funny if the siren went now wouldn't it?"

18   *Sunday Express, August 19, 1945*

Christine Keeler

The Keeler affair concerned the fact that she had been friendly at the same time with John Profumo, the British Secretary of State for War, and a Naval Attache at the Russian Embassy in London – a situation considered by the government to be a major security risk. Then, on June 20, the US Defense Secretary expressed concern that some US Air Force personnel may also have met Miss Keeler. President Kennedy arrived in London for an official visit on June 29.

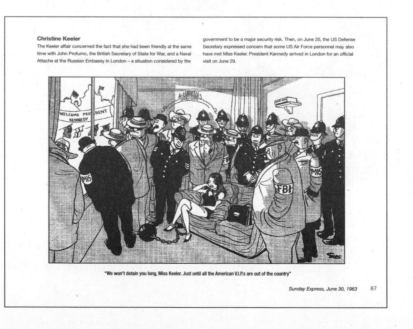

"We won't detain you long, Miss Keeler. Just until all the American V.I.P.s are out of the country"

Sunday Express, June 30, 1963   87